Dog Training

Everything You Need To Know To Raise The World's Best Dog From Puppy To Adulthood Using The Power Of Positive Reinforcement

(Training Your Dog Or Pup For Children And Adults)

Dirk-Bastian Konrad

TABLE OF CONTENT

Chapter 1: What Type Of Equipment Do You Require?.. 1

Chapter 2: Housebreaking Your Pup In Four Simple Steps 4

Chapter 3: Dachshund Puppy Training Continued Provide Your Dog With A Confinement Area: 10

Chapter 4: Adopt A Positive Attitude............................14

Chapter 5: The Ideal Collar For Both You And Your Dog During Walks, You Must Maintain Control Of Your Dog. 20

Chapter 6: How To Be An Excellent Dog Owner 22

Chapter 7: Teaching Your Canine To Cease Digging 33

Chapter 8: House Training Summary 40

Chapter 9: Managing The Dog's Hygiene Problems 43

Chapter 10: Unbroken Stage Of Remote Collar Training..49

Chapter 11: Methods To Encourage Cats And Dogs To Coexist..59

Chapter 12: Several Things Your Dog's Dna Sequence Can Inform You 68

Chapter 13: The Importance Of Selecting And Employing An Appropriate Dog Name........................75

Chapter 14: Why You Should Engage In Crate Training..82

Chapter 15: As You Instruct Your Mature Dog, ...91

Chapter 1: What Type Of Equipment Do You Require?

The owner must first decide what Determine the purpose and ultimate objective of the desired training based on the training equipment used. A training session is affected by numerous variables. A well-defined objective will encourage the dog and owner to work together to achieve it.

What You Must Have

Additionally, it is necessary to determine the type of training to be provided based on the established objective. If the sole purpose of the training is to establish boundaries for the dog, the owner should be able to identify a less aggressive training regimen that will accomplish the goal with the least amount of heartache on both sides. The required equipment should be limited to a leash, collar, and perhaps some tasty treats.

However, if the training is for a more specific purpose, such as breeding a champion show dog or a seeing eye dog, the required equipment will be vastly different and undeniably more suited to these objectives. The more difficult the objective, the more laser-focused the training equipment will be. This type of equipment is typically exclusive to well-known specialty stores stocked with a variety of specially designed dog training items. The majority of pet stores do not stock such custom-made items; therefore, it is essential to understand what is required before the actual sourcing process commences.

In addition to understanding how to operate and the purpose of the equipment to be purchased, the owner must also be able to do so. Failure to do so will not aid the training exercise and will only increase the dog's confusion and frustration, as the commands issued and the equipment used are insufficiently comparable.

Chapter 2: Housebreaking Your Pup In Four Simple Steps

The boy expressed confidence that he was not alone. I possess a puppy. Key Takeaway: Housebreaking your puppy contributes to the improvement of your relationship. You should not let the puppy outside until it has learned to use the restroom.

Your puppy must be housetrained using positive reinforcement, consistency, and perseverance. This exercise is designed to help your puppy develop some positive habits and establish a bond of affection. Between four and six months may be required for your dog to become housetrained. Some puppies could take up to a year to mature. Size may also play an important role.

A smaller puppy has a smaller bladder and a faster metabolism than a larger puppy. Therefore, a smaller puppy would require more frequent walks. The living conditions of the puppy should also be taken into account. Additionally, you may need to replace your dog's negative behaviours with positive ones. You must create and adhere to a schedule.

Be Patient

In addition, you will need perseverance and patience. Keep in mind that the dog you are interacting with is illiterate in human language. A puppy simply recognises your nonverbal cues and voice tone. In the process of training your dog, you will encounter obstacles. You should persevere in teaching the dog despite these obstacles. Your puppy will be fine as long as you maintain control over them. As soon as you observe signs that your puppy may need to use the restroom, you should take him outside and praise him for doing so. This will teach him a lesson.

When To Begin Toilet Training

Between 12 and 16 weeks of age, the puppy can begin housebreaking. At this age, the puppy can control his bowel and bladder functions. If you wait too long, housebreaking your puppy will take longer. If your puppy is accustomed to defecating in his cage, it will be more difficult to replace this behaviour with a positive one. The housetraining of your puppy will benefit from encouragement and rewards.

It is believed that restricting your puppy's access to space will aid in housebreaking. The puppy will not eliminate in its bed or food bowl.

Consequently, they would prefer to defecate outside. Here are some guidelines for housebreaking your puppy.

Create A schedule.

For your puppy, you must establish a feeding schedule and adhere to it. Do not allow the dog's bow to contain food! before or after meals. Take the puppy for a walk as soon as he awakens in the morning, after eating, when he awakens from a nap, and even after playing. Take him outside every hour or so to use the restroom.

In addition, he must be removed from the house before he falls asleep. Bring your dog to the same spot every time so he can defecate. The stench will also motivate him to do so. You must stay with him until he is able to use the restroom outside. Every time your dog defecates, you should either praise him or give him a treat. Additionally, a stroll may be enjoyable.

A container is an alternative option. However, do not confine your puppy for longer than two hours at a time. Allow him to spend only the night in the crate. If it is too large, the dog may use it as a toilet. If it were too small, he would not feel at ease. If you are unable to stay with your puppy while he is being trained, you will need to find someone to care for him and walk him while you are away from home. If you notice that your puppy is defecating in the crate, you should stop using it.

Common signs that your dog needs to go outside are sniffing the ground, barking, whining, circling, and scratching at the door. During the process of toilet training, accidents are inevitable. You must handle these occurrences professionally. Do not yell at or be disrespectful to your dog. Instead, clean the area thoroughly and take the dog outside. If you can keep an eye on your puppy, saying "no" as soon as you notice it about to urinate will also be helpful.

Chapter 3: Dachshund Puppy Training Continued Provide Your Dog With A Confinement Area:

Puppies frequently experiment with various behavioural patterns to determine their limits. It's important to give your dog a place to retreat, especially when you can't watch them. While you are away, they will be unable to roam the house and establish their own rules. Unsupervised, they will perceive that there is no authority over them and that they are free to do as they please.

Be as brief as possible: After you've taught your dog the fundamentals, try to use only one word for each command. The more concise your writing, the better. The simplest way to begin is with affirmative and negative statements. There may follow instructions such as sit, come, remain, and depart.

If the Dachshund dogs are not listening or are making a mess, do not yell at them, reprimand them, or hit them. Their poor behaviour is frequently the result of your inadequate instruction. Your unfavourable actions may have a lasting effect on your pet!

The Dachshund is an energetic and playful dog, so training should be brief. They may become easily distracted. Because children have such short attention spans, the key to success is frequent, brief training sessions.

f. Be dependable: dogs must be trained with consistency. Due to their inherent desire to be leaders, dachshunds will exploit any weaknesses in their owner's training techniques.

g. Make your pet social.

Your Dachshund's behaviour can only improve with early exposure to the outside world. There are numerous options for maximising your pet's socialisation.

Every time you take your dog for a walk outside of your yard, they become accustomed to a wide variety of unfamiliar objects. Unquestionably, acclimating children to the outside world has the potential to reduce behavioural fluctuations.

Refresh their senses by gradually exposing them to a variety of sounds and scents. This is one of the most effective methods for helping your dog overcome its fear of loud noises.

Salute one another: Introduce the Dachshund to new human and canine companions. When snuggling with a pet, individuals should be mindful to keep their hands visible to the dog.

Chapter 4: Adopt A Positive Attitude

When a dog is trained with punishment, it frequently develops a fear of its owner or trainer. Due to the uncertainty produced by the harness of the punishment, dogs that initially react negatively become desensitised and, in some cases, prefer to ignore the trainer or owner. Dogs that have been trained to obey out of pure fear of punishment are a horrifying and upsetting sight to behold, particularly for the more sensitive individual. Both the dog and the owner will suffer trauma as a result of this training method. The majority of dog owners will likely be unable to tolerate such a sight, which could make the dog even more confused.

In contrast, the positive reinforcement system utilised in training methods is frequently more popular and produces the desired results. The majority of the time, pets respond positively to rewards because they learn to associate particular behaviour patterns with pleasing the owner, which makes them acceptable. Even though most dogs enjoy receiving rewards and cooperating with their owners to achieve the desired outcomes, it is crucial to time these awards appropriately so that the dog associates the reward with a specific behaviour. In order for the dog to learn to associate a specific action with a reward, the reward must be delivered shortly after the appropriate behaviour. Failure to do so would result in confusion and prevent the dog from associating the behaviour with the reward.

chapter 1: The Problem With Failing to Train Your Dog

In order to have a harmonious relationship with one's dog, it is necessary to participate in training sessions. When keeping a dog as a pet, dog training is essential and often required for a variety of reasons.

Why Training Is Essential

The following are some of the reasons why training sessions are necessary:

• A misbehaving dog is not only a source of embarrassment for its owner, but also a very dangerous factor to consider. Untrained dogs will not readily obey commands, making them a hazard and a nuisance. If the owner is unable to keep the dog under control, particularly in the presence of children, the outcome of daily life in the unit could be unexpected and dangerous. Untrained dogs can also pose a threat to those in their vicinity. This type of dog will be unable to distinguish between right and wrong, contributing to upsetting destructive behaviour patterns such as digging up the garden, invading neighbouring areas, stealing things and chewing or playing with them, causing damage to the items, running wildly and causing chaos, and a variety of other equally upsetting destructive behaviour patterns. Obviously, this is not an ideal situation, as neither party will benefit and the lack of freedom may cause the dog distress.

Wrapping Up

Never assume that a dog is hopeless. Always keep in mind that a dog can be trained to do anything the owner desires with minimal effort. There is a reason dogs have been considered man's best friend for centuries. In most situations, they are incredibly devoted companions who will do anything to please their master, unless the master betrays the dog in any way. You can do it if you employ some of the aforementioned training methods. Best wishes!

Chapter 5: The Ideal Collar For Both You And Your Dog During Walks, You Must Maintain Control Of Your Dog.

A 4-to-6-foot-long, solid rope will be useful during your walk. You may choose any rope that feels comfortable to you. For long walks, calfskin or nylon rope chains with a short leash are optimal so you can exert rapid control over your dog in challenging situations.

A retractable leash is easy to hold and perfect for potty breaks or allowing your dog to wander on the chain. These are not ideal for dogs that pull excessively.

If you struggle with your dogs pulling on walks, a "no-pull harness" or body saddle could be a viable alternative. These outfits and a sturdy chain give you greater control over your dog while preparing.

Chapter 6: How To Be An Excellent Dog Owner

You have likely wondered at some point how to be a responsible dog owner. We have all contemplated this matter. We have all experienced the anxiety that accompanies thoughts of whether we're doing a good job and how we can improve domestic life for our furry best friends.

Take a breath with your diaphragm. The fact that you are reading about how to be a good dog parent indicates your devotion to your pet. And if you're reading a book about dog training, you're probably already doing an excellent job. However, you can always improve in some ways.

Sharing your life with your puppy is a wonderful experience and feeling. Don't be surprised if you feel that your dog is an integral part of your family and life; she makes you laugh, keeps you company, and shares adventures.

You owe it to your best friend to understand what she requires from you in order to be healthy and happy, and to be there for her in the appropriate ways. This positively improves both of your lives.

So, you've just brought your beloved furry companion home. What are your responsibilities, and how can you fulfil them in a safe and effective manner?

First, you must comprehend what it means to be a good dog parent. What does it mean to be a good dog owner? is an existential question in and of itself. I believe there is no objectively correct answer.

Each dog owner I spoke with had a unique perspective on what it means to be a responsible pet parent. As you're doing now, some believe a good dog owner takes the time to learn as much as possible about dog ownership, care, and training.

Others argued that being a good dog parent requires setting expectations and boundaries, establishing a routine and schedule, and balancing this with positive reinforcement and love. It takes structure and positive reinforcement to build trust between dogs and their owners.

The most important aspect of being a good dog owner is putting your pet's needs before your own. While you may wish to assert your leadership as the pack's alpha, you should never disregard how your dog feels about certain things. For example, if your dog does not like a specific collar, you should not force her to wear it. That will make her miserable.

There is no one right way to be a good pet parent, but there are certain things that all good parents do. And doing so can make training your dog extraordinarily stress-free for everyone involved.

Here are methods for making your dog happy and being a responsible owner.

Safety and Security First - Legal and Medical Obligations

Automobile travel with a dog necessitates microchipping. Ensure that your dog is properly restrained in a vehicle to prevent them from distracting you or injuring you or themselves, especially in situations involving sudden stops.

The safest methods for restraining your dog in a vehicle include a seat belt harness, a dog cage, a dog carrier, a dog guard, and so on.

The obligation does not end there. Being a responsible dog owner necessitates: Carrying poop bags with you at all times. Thus, you will always be prepared to clean up after your furry friend, and you can avoid penalties for leaving your dog's waste behind.

If you cannot locate a dog poop bin, you may dispose of it in a regular trash can.

Resist the urge to leave your dog unattended in public places. Even if she is securely leashed, leaving a dog unattended could result in her being injured or stolen. Plan ahead to ensure that you can bring your dog with you wherever you go.

You owe your dog excellent veterinary care, as it is essential for her health.

Vaccinations should be up-to-date, and regular checkups should be performed. If you want your dog to live a long and healthy life, you must do so. On average, puppies are vaccinated between 6 and 8 weeks of age; however, your licenced veterinarian will determine the proper protocol for your puppy.

You may feel as though your dog is your child; this is a healthy sentiment. Still, your dog is not human; she cannot communicate when she is ill. Therefore, you owe it to her to be as aware as possible of her health.

In addition to routine health examinations, you should know your furry best friend well enough to recognise changes in appearance or behaviour that may indicate an underlying medical condition. Your medical responsibilities include having the means to pay for your dog's veterinary care, should the need arise.

Grooming

If you've never raised a puppy, it's easy to succumb to their adorableness. Obviously, this disillusions you into ignoring grooming requirements prior to acquiring a specific breed dog. Don't be disheartened if you discover that your dog's breed has specific grooming requirements. Different dog breeds have distinct grooming requirements.

You are the dog's parent, so it is your responsibility to be aware of and updated on your dog's grooming requirements. Regardless of breed, all dogs need regular baths and nail trims. Depending on their amount of fur, some dogs require combing, brushing, and haircuts.

Regular visits to a professional groomer may be necessary to help your dog maintain her best appearance if you desire a dog that is always well-groomed and attractive.

Feeding

Good dog parents take the time to learn as much as possible about their pup's dietary requirements, which, as you may already be aware, vary by breed. To maintain their health, dogs require an adequate amount of high-quality food containing the proper ratio of essential nutrients and calories. You do not want your puppy to consume too many fillers. You should observe your dog to determine if her diet needs to be altered.

This is crucial if you want your dog's weight and coat to remain healthy. Feed your dog a variety of foods to keep her anticipating mealtimes.

Exercising

Do you exercise? Your dog will require exercise if this is true. And if you do not, who better to begin with than your furry companion? Even seemingly low-energy dogs require physical activity.

Depending on the breed, daily short walks around the neighbourhood may suffice as exercise. Or it could mean engaging in vigorous activities such as hiking after work. To be a good dog owner, you can begin by learning your dog's exercise requirements and incorporating them into your daily routine.

Lastly, it may entail walking your pet to the park twice daily for vigorous play that can burn off a young dog's abundant energy.

Training

As I've stated multiple times, training is the best thing you can do as a responsible dog owner for your puppy. To thrive, canines require routine and structure. You are inspired by your friend's well-trained dog to acquire one for yourself. A well-trained dog is a happy dog, and that dog's happiness can spread to the owner and others.

However, you are aware that training is not the only factor that makes you a responsible owner. Additionally, training is the most effective way to keep your dog safe. If you have control over your pet, you can keep her away from potentially dangerous situations. And well-mannered dogs are a reflection of the community of dog owners, making public spaces more accessible to dogs.

Being a good and responsible dog parent includes treating your dog like a vital family member.

Obviously, no one needs to inform you that this love must be unconditional.

Do not expect a perfect dog; they do not exist outside of the movies. Realistically, your dog will act out and misbehave from time to time. That shouldn't diminish your love for her, whether your life together is perfect or you're experiencing difficulties.

Chapter 7: Teaching Your Canine To Cease Digging

Sand excavation is a beneficial exercise.

Have you ever returned home to find your newly planted flowers dispersed throughout the backyard? One of your lawnmower's wheels went into a dog hole, causing damage. Have you ever discovered a newly dug hole in your yard at midnight?

Those with dogs that dig up their yards are not alone. One of the most common complaints about dogs is that they dig; it is not an easy or simple problem to solve, but it is solvable.

There are as many methods for halting digging as there are causes for it.

How Can I Prevent My Canine from Digging?

If you are unable to offer your dog a job, you should at least ensure she receives sufficient exercise. My dog often falls asleep after our morning walks, and digging is the last thing she wants to do!

Frozen Kong toys can be stuffed with kibble or peanut butter. Chewing and licking a toy prevents a dog from digging.

Your dog will be much more likely to dig if she is confined to the backyard whenever there is activity inside the house. If she views the backyard as a playground, she will dig less.

Basically consider alternative options if your dog is attempting to cool off. A possible solution would be to give her a wading pool. Another alternative is to build a sandbox for your dog. Your dog will end the day covered in mud or sand, but will most likely refrain from digging.

This is essential for dogs attempting to escape by digging. Neutering is an excellent option for all animals.

This is the best option for all dogs, but it is essential for hunting dogs (like Fox Terriers and Dachshunds) that enjoy "going to ground." Either designate a play area or build a sandbox and bury her favourite toys within it. As soon as she begins to dig, you could lavish her with compliments. Since I dug a hole for my dog to use as a watering hole in the tropics, she never digs outside of the designated area.

This is a last resort after all other methods have failed, but it may work. When my dog was a puppy, she dug holes in front of the door despite having a good place to dig. To prevent this, you can place her stool in the hole and then cover it with sand. The following time she digs there, she finds her stool first. Combining this strategy with other options, such as providing your dog with a sandbox, will ensure its success. This will not stop your dog from digging, but it will cause him to dig elsewhere.

A dog that is bored will often dig to pass the time.

Small Dogs Dig Big Holes, Too

Even Westies and Yorkies were bred to dig. A determined small dog can dig up a yard as effectively as a large dog.

This item is at the top of the list for good reason. Since the majority of dogs are unemployed, they must find something to do. When dogs dig in the garden, for example, they are simply imitating human behaviour. Digging is a good way for a bored dog to kill time.

In the winter, when the ground is frozen, digging is not a problem, but in the summer, dogs dig holes to cool themselves. Long-haired breeds are not adapted to live in warm climates because they experience extreme discomfort.

New toys, old bones, and all types of beloved items must be buried, regardless of the reason.

a natural reason for digging. A dog may be unsuccessful multiple times, but he will continue to dig if he finds food even once.

Objects buried must be unearthed. On occasion, dogs experience "lost keys syndrome" and forget where they buried their favourite bone or toy. They need to look everywhere for it.

This is a common problem with certain dogs, especially intact males. Some dogs must flee if they are not taken outside frequently enough. Typically along the fence line, but occasionally quite deep.

Some canines will dig regardless of your efforts.

Remember that your dog's natural instinct is to dig.

Do not become angry if your dog digs. If you chose to acquire a Dachshund, it should not come as a surprise that she enjoys digging; this is to be expected. Try implementing some of the presented solutions, and your problems will diminish.

Reduced but not eliminated! Nevertheless, regardless of how well you train them, dogs enjoy digging!

Westies make excellent guard dogs, but they can be trained to refrain from excessive barking.

Chapter 8: House Training Summary

Although it may appear cruel to expect an animal to "hold it" when humans can simply locate a restroom, it will be beneficial for the animal to establish a routine.

This will assist in easing the burden of an anxious pet and owner.

No More Accidents

The following steps can be taken to reduce the number of "accidents" that occur while housebreaking the animal:

- Consistency is required when identifying a specific area that the owner hopes the dog will eventually recognise as the bathroom. Observing when the dog is likely to require a bathroom break and immediately taking the animal to the designated area until the deed is complete will teach the dog the significance of the designated area. Additionally, lavishing praise upon completion will help reinforce the concept of taking the dog to the designated area.

• Taking the time to comprehend the dog is also an essential component of dog training. Most dogs cannot associate disapproval with the act of defecating because their owners rarely catch them in the act. The owner's reprimand is typically administered only after the "accident" or mess has been discovered. Therefore, the animal will eventually associate disapproval with the resulting mess and not with the act of defecation itself. To ensure the animal understands the "misdemeanour," it is crucial for the owner to express disapproval at the moment the action is committed, as opposed to afterward. Once this is determined, both parties can collaborate to find an as stress-free a solution as possible. As the animal's capacity to comprehend things is limited, the owner must always remember not to exert excessive pressure on it.

Chapter 9: Managing The Dog's Hygiene Problems

Your adorable, snoozing dog is one of the world's greatest attractions, as he appears to be completely unfazed and at peace. Even more endearing is when he yawns, opens his mouth, stands slowly, and stares you for a long time. Through the glimmer in his eyes, you can see how small and green the puppy is, prompting you to give him a lengthy and substantial hug. However, after you embrace him, you detect a pungent odour on your skin. You then realise that the dog has defecated on your arms. And a few moments later, he begins to bite as though he is biting his toy, and now it is twice as difficult.

This is how the first-rate images in our minds become obscured by the fact that dogs have grave problems we must address immediately as soon as they are with us. Primarily, the problem for the majority of dog owners, as well as everyone else, is when their dogs defecate in random areas of the house. This is the dependency that the majority of people need a solution for, because nobody wants their home's flooring to be ruined by their dog's faeces.

This is where house training enters the picture. The key to effective house training is consistency and endurance. Routine refers to the recurrence of taking the dog for a walk outside or to a designated area after he finishes eating. The instructor must be able to praise the dog for defecating or urinating in the designated area, as this will send the dog the message that his actions were acceptable.

However, patience requires that dogs be tolerated if they are unable to reach the course immediately. It can be repeated numerous times using the same words, gestures, and praise device for as long as it is necessary. You should simply wait until the dog is familiar with the scent of the designated area he is typically introduced to when he is required to defecate. You must be consistent with the praise you give your dog when he performs a task correctly and the response he receives when he does not make a mistake. All of them must be consistent.

The fundamentals of a dog's hygiene hinge on how you attend to his basic sanitary requirements. As soon as possible, the puppy must be accustomed to being brushed and bathed. A puppy will remember these activities as things he looks forward to if he is introduced to them early in his life at your home. As puppies may also initially feel normal with water contact on their entire body, this can be challenging. Puppies can also look forward to brushing and bathing each subsequent day with enthusiasm if they are introduced to these activities in a fun and careful manner.

In terms of the showering system, it is preferable to permit your dog to settle in first. After he has calmed down, you can place him in a small bath and begin brushing him. However, not all puppies have long hair. It may also depend on one breed over another. Additionally, it is acceptable to converse with your dog while shampooing him. In addition, it is during these occasions that the dog feels closer to his instructor. Initially, it may be very difficult due to the small dog's potential resistance. In extreme circumstances, you may need assistance from another person to wash the dog.

The same principle applies to brushing the dog's teeth and clipping his claws. Initially, the domestic dog can also refuse and struggle further. However, if these activities are introduced to a puppy early on, he will become accustomed to them. You simply need to use the same vocabulary when commanding the dog, along with reasonable care when he resists, appropriate use of the praise device when he complies, and, of course, persistence when he does not initially comply with your commands.

A new instructor who has experienced what a dog goes through is superior to a dog trainer with years of experience, but who lacks empathy.

Chapter 10: Unbroken Stage Of Remote Collar Training

How do you know when a dog is ready for the leash to be removed?

The purpose of training a dog with an e-collar is to enable you to run the dog off leash while remaining confident that you can maintain control when necessary.

But how do you know when the dog is truly ready for the leash or long line to be removed?

If you go from e-collar training on leash and assisting the dog in doing things correctly to completely unclipping the leash, your dog may not be prepared.

Working on obedience at the beginning of the training process is the best way to ensure that the dog will exhibit the desired behaviour. The leash serves as a means of applying pressure to assist the dog in performing a recall or heel turn. It is a way to keep the dog's attention on the trainer and cues when teaching Sit, Place, or Down. However, it can also be a srutsh. If we forget to wean the dog off the leash, the dog will never fully understand the response to e-collar stimulation in the absence of the leash.

That is why it is essential to undergo a transition after training and work with a dragline. A draglne is precisely what it sounds like: a dog dragging a leash or long line with a flat buskle sollar.

Having a line dragging from the dog gives you a good indication of whether or not the dog has difficulty following through with only electronic pressure. At any time the dog demonstrates how confusion, you can rsk up the line and assist in guiding the dog towards the desired behaviour. The line is assisting you, just as it did in the early phase of surveying, but you are no longer holding it in your hand or monitoring its progress.

Due to the fact that the line is generally dragging and is only picked up and used as needed, the dog has the opportunity to demonstrate to you his level of comprehension. If you are frequently crossing the line to assist, the dog is not yet ready to work off leash. If you are extremely unlikely to ever cross the line and have put in the work to generalise to a variety of situations and outcomes, then your dog is ready to go without a leash. With the e-collar on, you now possess total control.

To ensure that the use of the leash and the tension attached to it do not become a crutch. Too frequently, individuals struggle with having a long leash during training. Constant tension can be harmful to the dog, but when the leash is removed, the tension disappears. Fdo may be unable to rerond sorrestlu. Allowing the leash to dangle allows the handler to develop other skills for assisting the dog in understanding, but it is still available as a backup.

An additional step that may be taken is shortening the line by removing portions of rerodsallu. This indicates a gradual reduction in the amount of weight the dog is carrying. Rather than letting your dog go "cold turkey" with no leash, you should gradually shorten the leash until only a small tab remains attached to the collar.

Importantly, you must recognise that your dog is intelligent enough to recognise when a leash or line is no longer attached to you.

If you train and take intermediate steps using a drag line, you will have a greater chance of achieving the desired off-road dependability.

Utilizing Food And Treats In Addition To The Electronic Collar

One of the most straightforward ways for an average trainer to teach a dog the meaning of a verbal cue is through lure and reward training.

The concept behind Lure and Reward is extremely simple. The body of an animal follows where the nose goes. When you basically consider a Hound, a very vivid image comes to mind. The scent of something intriguing led the dog to perform a variety of actions, including walking along a path, crawling under a low fence line, and standing on its hind legs to investigate what was in the tree.

You can use your dog's keen sense of smell and desire for something tasty to teach the behaviour of simple changes in body position, such as Sit, Stand, and Down, very quickly. Once the dog grasps the concept, you can transfer it to the e-collar so that you can later build the desired relationship.

The key to using food effectively in training is learning how to do so correctly. Sounds familiar, right? Learning how to use each of our dog training tools effectively is the key to success!

Properly, you should ONLY use it as a lure for a few returns. As soon as the dog grasps the concept of following your hand, you relocate the food. Reward the dog with an easily accessible treat, such as a treat pouch or treat bag, AFTER it has successfully followed your hand to the desired position. Now you have created a hand signal that can be used independently or in conjunction with your verbal commands.

Eventually, you can wean your dog off hand signals as well, so that only verbal commands will elicit a response from your dog. The exception to this is dogs that can hear infrared. For these dogs, we will continue to use hand signals and add tasty treats in order to immunise them for life.

Early on in the training, Rose began to utilise the treat reward consistently. This is what creates a dog that responds enthusiastically but is not dependent on a brbe. Basically consider yourself a slot machine. You rau out occasionally, sometimes a little, occasionally a great deal. A large payout in terms of treats is several as opposed to one, or something more luxurious, such as a bite of chicken as opposed to a bowl of cereal. Don't overfeed your dog simply because you had a single training session. I have witnessed trainers whose dogs vomit at the end of class because they are so overfed. This is an improper use of food rewards, and the dog will never work unless he is bribed.

The use of treats and food makes behaviour modification very early and natural. I ensourage it. If using treats is truly against your diet, use a tou instead. Use food, toys, and praise intermittently as rewards, and you will never be without a way to show your dog that he has performed admirably.

A you rrogre uou do not need to reward the dog for every single sorrest response, but I urest we all enjoy eventually receiving a paycheck for our efforts. For your dog, this may entail the continued use of treats, a game of tug-of-war, a belly rub and a kind word, or even permission to chase the squirrel!

Chapter 11: Methods To Encourage Cats And Dogs To Coexist

Everyone has heard the idiom "fighting like cats and dogs," but this does not have to be the case for your pets with a little effort. To assist you, we have compiled a list of seven things you can do to ensure that your dogs live happily together.

RAISING THEM JOINTLY

One of the simplest ways to encourage cats and dogs to live together is to raise them together. Puppies are more trainable and less confident than adult dogs, so they are more likely to allow their feline companions to assume the alpha position in the family. Obviously, this is not always possible, so proceed if you must introduce mature cats and dogs.

DOCUMENT YOUR CAT'S TERRITORY

Your cat must have a designated space in your home. Having this space will be especially important when introducing your pets for the first time, but it will also serve as a sanctuary they can retreat to when they need some peace and quiet.

Don't worry about restricting your dog's access to space if you reside in a small dwelling. Because cats are natural climbers, you can utilise any vertical space in your home, be it a cat tree or a recently built bookshelf. Both of these settings are ideal for your cat to observe your dog from a safe distance.

INTRODUCE THEIR MERCHANDISE PRIOR TO INTRODUCING THEM

Before beginning the face-to-face meeting, it's a good idea to introduce the other party's dog's bedding and toys. By doing so, each pet will have the opportunity to become acquainted with the other, satisfy their curiosity, and avoid any potential conflicts that could arise if they explored while the other was nearby. Animals use their sense of smell to acclimatise themselves to new objects; therefore, each pet will be able to satisfy its curiosity, and you can avoid any potential conflicts that may arise if one is examined while the other is nearby.

SPEED UP THE INTRODUCTION

When the time comes for your cat and dog to meet in person, it is imperative to proceed with caution. As with people, first impressions are crucial. And food can be a great tool for making a positive first impression and ensuring everything goes smoothly. Mealtime is the best time for your pets to interact. Feed your dogs their first meal on the opposite side of a closed door.

Thus, they will be unable to see one another, but will still be able to smell one another and begin to form positive associations between delicious food and their new companion. Continue for as long as you deem necessary – a few days to a few weeks, depending on how your pets respond – and then gradually introduce a visual component. A simple way to achieve this is to feed your dogs in the same room while keeping them on leashes. Eventually, you will be able to remove all barriers between them, and they will be able to coexist peacefully.

KEEP THINGS EQUAL

Jealousy and resentment over toys, treats, and attention can have a significant impact on the relationship between a cat and a dog, so it is essential to maintain parity. This entails ensuring that your dogs have equal access to toys and treats so that things remain fair.

However, this equality extends beyond just physical objects; the time spent with them should also be equal. For instance, if you always make a fuss over your dog when you get home, your cat will eventually catch up and may find ways to express their discontent with the inequity — or vice versa.

TRAIN YOUR DOG WELL

Before any introductions are made, your dog must be well-versed in basic commands such as sit, stay, down, drop, and leave it. Because they will be able to remain calm when meeting the cat, introductions will go more smoothly the more thoroughly they understand these instructions.

When your dog is playing with your cat, you must redirect any undesirable behaviours, such as rough play and excessive barking. Try distracting them with another activity or command and letting them "reset" before returning to your cat instead of criticising them. The more pleasant you can keep the situation, the more positive associations they will form not only with your cat, but with every cat they encounter.

SEPARATE THEIR PROPERTY

Regardless of how well they get along after their initial encounter, it is prudent to give them each their own space. This includes providing a separate location for your cat's litter box. Unfortunately, some dogs tend to be excessively curious about the contents of litter boxes. If your dog attempts to approach your cat while it is using the litter box, your cat may feel threatened, and if this occurs repeatedly, they may avoid using the litter box for elimination.

The same is true of food. Feeding your dogs in different locations reduces the likelihood of food aggression incidents. It also ensures that each pet can eat at their own pace without feeling rushed. The most important thing to remember when introducing your cats and dogs is that they are all unique; what works for one may not work for another. If you're trying to help your dogs form a bond, your veterinarian is the best person to consult. They will be able to provide you with specialised advice or connect you with a behavioural specialist. However, with a little patience, your cat and dog will cohabitate peacefully in almost all cases!

Chapter 12: Several Things Your Dog's Dna Sequence Can Inform You

Many individuals are interested in learning about their familu trees, ethnic background, or medical rrediroition, but what about their dog? Just given the large number of stray and abandoned dogs who end up in shelters, it is not surprising that DNA testing for dogs has become increasingly popular. Dog DNA kits, such as those offered by Embark, Wisdom Panel, and Royal Canin, have recently become a popular option for animal lovers, and breed reveals and guessing games have become fairly common on social media.

However, these genetic test kits can provide you with more information than just your dog's breed. Using a DNA test, here are five things that can be determined about your dog:

Informational concerning the Breed and Its Traits

The discovery that their newly adopted dog is a mix of breeds is typically the most exciting aspect for new dog owners. The results of a DNA test will reveal your dog's breed composition as a percentage based on a database containing between 250 and 350 dog breeds. You will be able to obtain additional information on each of the breeds from which your puppy is bred, such as their characteristics, appearances, histories, interesting facts, and related breed information.

Discovering your dog's ancestry and creating a "family tree" for them (identifying the breeds of their parents, grandparents, and great-grandparents) is another responsibility. Even for purebred dogs, this can confirm that their family tree extends back several generations. s.

Other fascinating breed information that can be obtained with various kits includes genetis age, characteristics, Wolfine (ancient genetic traits), maternal line (finding out which locations the mother's ancestry can be traced), and genetis age. This may include the colour and length of the grain, the size of the bodu, the amount of shedding, the colour of the eue, the genetic variety (inbreeding), and even the capacity to withstand high altitude!

2. Dangerous to One's Health and Gene Pool

If you are interested in learning about the hereditary health risks associated with your dog, you may want to basically consider purchasing a kit that includes a health screening. These health kits have the ability to screen for more than 150 hereditary diseases for which your dog may be "at risk" or a "carrier" depending on the breed mix. It has the potential to diagnose diseases such as glaucoma and von Willebrand disease, as well as breed-specific conditions such as golden retriever muscular dystrophy.

Additionally, you can have your dog tested for the MDR1 gene, also known as the multidrug resistance gene. If your dog carries this gene, he or she may have severe reactions to several common medications.

If your dog tests positive for any of these diseases or mutations, you will be able to take preventative action as a dog owner. As your dog ages, you will have a greater understanding of the signs and symptoms to look for, and you will be able to involve your dog's veterinarian for more comprehensive care.

3. Resmmendations Regarding Your Weight and Diet, DNA Testing Can Provide Useful Information information about the size of your dog's cranium. The results can provide you with an estimate of your dog's adult weight, which is useful if you are assessing your pet at this age. You may also receive a recommendation for a healthy weight range, which will provide you with an idea of how much your dog should weigh to maintain his or her health.

There are additional nutritional considerations that come with some DNA testing, and they depend on your dog's size and breed mix. The inclusion of recommended nutrient and mineral is beneficial to the digestive system, joints, skin, and soat mau. This can make it easier for you, along with the advice of your veterinarian, to select the appropriate diet and supplements for your dog.

4. Discard a Portion of Your Dog's Relative

What an incredible adventure it would be to lose your dog's long-lost sister! Through the use of the Doggy DNA Relative Finder, you will be able to make contact with other dogs that share DNA with your dog. Even if a relative signs up for the registry after you have completed the exam for your dog, you will continue to receive notifications about their participation because updates are sent on an ongoing basis. Due to this remarkable functionality, there have even been some wonderful reunions in the past. Currently, only Embark is equipped with this capability.

5. Participation in Research

Now, this is not something you receive from the DNA test; rather, it is something you can provide. When you send in your dog's DNA, you are also contributing to fascinating studies on the genetics of animals used in veterinary medicine. Veterinaru rrofeional are gaining a better understanding of topics such as canine obesity, diseases, behavioural issues, ageing, and preventive care as a result of this research. In addition, as time passes, you may gain access to new activities and experiences!

Chapter 13: The Importance Of Selecting And Employing An Appropriate Dog Name

Your dog's name is a crucial identifier for communicating with them. For your dog, it means "pay attention to whoever said my name," and if you want it to perform at its best, it should mean "listening to whoever said my name results in tasty treats!"

If you adopt a domestic dog from a breeder or a shelter, you may be able to give them any name you desire. However, I suggest you carefully basically consider the call you make. There are personal factors to basically consider in addition to practical factors.

Choose a name with a maximum number of syllables; one that is succinct and distinct. Princess Margaret is a great name for a dog, but due to its age, it may be significantly less effective. I might suggest that you train Princess, Maggie, or Mags. Puppies find it easier to comprehend names that are brief.

Choose a name that is unique and doesn't resemble a verbal cue you use for training or a member of the family member's name. For instance, "Clown" is an excellent moniker for a dog who is constantly goofy. Nonetheless, it sounds identical to the verbal cue "Down." That should make things confusing for your beloved Clown, so "Goofy" might be a better name. Avoid choosing a name that is similar to the names of other animals or members of your household. Having a Joe, a Moe, and a Beau all living in the same residence would be very confusing.

In addition, these names sound like "No," a word that the majority of dog owners use far too frequently.

If you follow the aforementioned guidelines, you can give your dog any name you desire.

Most older puppies we bring into our homes will already have a name. If the dog already responds enthusiastically to their call, hold the call, even if you're not fond of it. We observed our dog Shed as she turned five years old. We have been instructed that the term is an abbreviation for "Sh**head," which is no longer merely a nickname. However, Shed responded to "Shed" with enthusiasm and pleasure, so that it would remain her name.

Our dog Muppy was discovered as a stray in Mississippi when she was approximately 18 months old. She became pregnant and moved into a foster home for eight weeks, where she was just given the name Marlene. She became Molly somewhere between her foster home and her transfer to a rescue in New Hampshire. When she was just given to us, she did not answer either of our calls, so it took us some time to recognise her personality. Approximately one week later, she became "Muppy." She has been with us for six years, and everyone agrees that her name is appropriate.

It's your dog, so you're free to name her whatever you like; however, other members of your immediate family may also wish to weigh in on the matter. As stated previously, I suggest the adults have veto power to ensure that the decision is reasonable. For instance, it is entirely possible for a child to believe that "Mister Fluffy Pants" is the most pleasant name ever, but you should meet them halfway. Get the dog something labelled "Mister Fluffy Pants" (a bowl, a bed, a collar, etc.), but agree to use something shorter for training; perhaps "Fluffy." The name you choose for your dog's ID tag and microchip should be the same as the one you use in everyday life.

If you received your puppy from a breeder in exchange for signing in the muddle, the breeder could have input on the puppy's registered name. Tikken, our Golden Retriever, was bred by means of Mariner Kennels and was born on Martin Luther King Day. Mariner considered her to be a member of the "Freedom" muddle and desired that her registered name include both "Mariner" and "Freedom." Our desire for Tikken's registered name to be "Marine Freedom Fighter" led us to the name Marine Freedom Fighter.

Do not feel compelled to choose a name for your dog on the first day or earlier than bringing it home. However, recognise that you no longer need to attend for too long. From the moment my wife and I met Gus, even before we decided to bring him home, we knew he was a "Gus." The longer he remained with us, the greater our satisfaction with our choice grew. With Tikken, Dulcie, and Muppy, it took some time to select a desirable name.

NEVER use your dog's name in a frustrated or angry manner. Even a single instance of this behaviour could cause your dog to avoid you. This error can be extremely difficult to correct.

Chapter 14: Why You Should Engage In Crate Training

Whether crate training is a good or bad way to help train a puppy, the camps appear to be evenly divided. I believe that the majority of unfavourable comments are a result of using the crate as a form of punishment. I believe that the crate can be an invaluable tool for training your puppy, and that if used properly, your dog will enjoy its crate.

A crate provides a puppy with, if you will, comfort and security, his own safe space in which he can relax and, of course, sleep at night.

It helps tremendously with housebreaking by rapidly teaching them to hold their urine for longer periods of time.

When people come to the door and your puppy becomes overly excited, it can be used to calm down before being properly introduced to your guests.

It also teaches your puppy that crates are normal, so they remain calm and relaxed when they need to be in a kennel for an extended period, such as at the veterinarian, groomer, or when you are away on vacation and they must stay in a boarding kennel.

Here are some guidelines for crate training. When your puppy is resting during the day in their crate, which is their safe space, leave them alone. Do not subject your puppy to interference from children, other animals, etc.

Do provide an easily accessible location for the crate, preferably in a quieter area where there is not constant noise. I am aware that when humans want to take a nap, nothing is worse than being constantly awoken by noise and commotion and waking up feeling unrested and irritated. Keep this in mind when your dog goes to sleep.

Never use force when placing your puppy in its crate. If necessary, place a treat at the back of the crate so they will enter on their own to get it.

Which box is the correct one?

When it comes to crates, you have a few options; the two most popular are the plastic hard shell crates, which are more versatile because they are great for transporting your puppy in the car, and the wire mesh crates, which are typically collapsible and have a divider.

To me, it doesn't really matter which one you choose; however, keep in mind that if you choose the plastic style, you may need to purchase a new one as they grow, whereas with the mesh style, make sure it has a divider and purchase one for their adult size. As your puppy grows, adjust the divider to provide it with the proper amount of space inside the crate. Size is the most crucial factor...yes, size does matter!

The crate should be large enough for your puppy to stand up, turn around, and stretch out with its legs extended. Therefore, if your puppy's height from floor to shoulder is 12 inches, you would want a crate that is perhaps a few inches wider than 15 or 16 inches. If the crate is too large, the likelihood of your puppy defecating or urinating in it dramatically increases, as they will defecate in one end and sleep in the other.

You can add additional comfort to the crate by providing a bed or blanket of the appropriate size. Just make sure they're not chewing them, as this would make the space too hot for them. Additionally, you will need to regularly clean the bedding and the crate itself. My dog utilised to awaken as soon as the sun rose. I found that placing a blanket over the crate so that it was always dark helped a great deal, and then I was the one who had to wake her up.

Instruct your puppy to adore their new crate

How can we teach our puppies to adore their crate? The answer is fairly obvious. We will instruct them to associate only positive memories with it. Only good things occur when they are in their crate. Ideally, you want your puppy to enjoy going into their crate because it will make everything we've discussed thus far much easier.

The majority of puppies are food-motivated, so we will take advantage of this. While your puppy is learning to enjoy its crate, we will feed it all of its meals in it. At mealtimes, I would remove any bedding because it can become messy, especially if you are feeding a wet or raw food. During the first few days, you will need to alternate between opening and closing the door for a few minutes while they are eating. You will want to gradually leave the crate door closed for longer and longer periods of time until it is completely shut.

When it is time to give them a treat or something to chew on, do so in their crate. Ideal is a chew stick that is edible and lasts a long time. Basically consider a bully stick or deer antler, or something similar. Never provide your dog with rawhide. There may be trace amounts of toxic chemicals in rawhide. Large pieces of rawhide can also cause digestive irritation, choking, and blockages if ingested by a puppy. Depending on the size and location of the obstruction, it may be necessary to perform surgery on your dog to remove it. If the obstruction is not removed in a timely manner, it can even be fatal.

We want them to remain in their crate while they are eating or chewing their treat. Before they begin to whine or bark, open the door and allow them to leave if they wish after they have completed their task.

As humans, we are accustomed to not wanting them to whine and bark, so we open the door and let them out before they begin to whimper and bark. Unfortunately, we are currently rewarding undesirable or undesirable behaviour. Your dog will learn that whining and persisting will earn them what they want.

With crate training or any other type of training, we want to only reward good behaviour. Ideal positions are sitting or lying down quietly and calmly.

Any puppy or dog can be crate-trained and taught to love their crate; however, it is your responsibility to be consistent, persistent, and never give up.

Chapter 15: As You Instruct Your Mature Dog,

If you continue training past the beginner level, certain conditions are inevitable: you will have formal training sessions with your dog in which you feel happy and satisfied.

You will experience poor training classes with your dog, leaving you frustrated and angry. (attempt to prevent the dog from noticing it.)

You may make numerous mistakes during your education.

You will receive corrections from your instructors, albeit a few days later than others.

Occasionally, you may feel that "you understand better" and no longer adhere to your teachers' recommendations.

You will find yourself comparing your dog unfavourably to others in the class.

You occasionally find yourself irritated with your instructors and classmates.

There may be times when you want to quit, but you don't. Because you know in your heart that you and your dog can do it.

There may be some physical games that you do not practice as frequently as others because you dislike them.

There will be times when you question whether dog training fits into your lifestyle.

I recognize. I was a student significantly longer than I was a teacher. Nonetheless,

I am a student. Everyone who trains has experienced these feelings at some point. a few uplifting phrases:

You can obtain a degree if you desire it with sufficient intensity. Your determination is significantly more potent than even the hardest dog.

No error you make while training your dog is ever irreversible. Puppies are thoroughly retrained.

Your second and 0.33 dogs may be superior to your first. Every dog will teach you how to be a more effective trainer.

With each conflict you face in school, whether with your dog, your teacher, your classmates, or your spouse, you gain knowledge. Obviously, you cannot understand it in time.

The mother of invention is necessity, especially in dog training.

Dog training is an exceptional and unique sport. It encompasses all ages, all existences, all economies, and both genders. It stimulates both the mind and the body. It teaches both sportsmanship and compassion. Dog training improves resiliency and imparts knowledge about yourself, your dog, and others. Dog training takes on a new perspective after the novice stage. Basically consider the issues and difficulties as a boon. Provide the conflicts as opportunities for mastery.

www.ingramcontent.com/pod-product-compliance
Lightning Source LLC
Chambersburg PA
CBHW050306120526
44590CB00016B/2514